C000201883

Comedians may co

And some I'd like to see

Not 'cos it means less competition

But because they do stoop low

Some today lay it on with a trowel

They love to 'F' and 'blind'

But much as I do - in private of course

They're not really quite my kind.

Within these pages are the gems

That came from the Master's mouth

Not an 'F' or a 'blind' but just

Great stuff from Himself!

PRESIDENT

MMAS

KEN DODD

"Congratulations to the Max Miller Appreciation Society for producing Max Miller's NEW BLUE BOOK!

It's an excellent way to remember a great comedian. I look forward to reading it and exercising my chuckle muscles. Happiness to everyone."

Yours tattyphilariously,

Ken Dodd

"Miller's the name, lady"
"You can't help liking him!"
"It's all clever stuff; no rubbish!"
"Now, there's a funny thing!"
"I don't care what I say, do I?"
"There'll never be another!"

We asked the chairman of the Max Miller Appreciation Society, Averil Older, why she loves Brighton (and Hove – actually!)

Well, I can't claim to have been born in this wonderful city, but I have lived here for over sixty years. How old does that make me, I hear you all shout – cheeky!

I was always aware that many star names have made their home here over the years – just look at the front of any of our buses. A good number of their houses are now commemorated by blue plaques, including Max's, of course, but he was special!

Born in the city in 1894, Max will always be regarded as 'one of our own', and I often meet residents and visitors who have stories to tell of their Max moments. For the last twenty years I have lived in Hove, and having read John East's biography of Max, I realised that my home was within two minutes' walk of one of the schools the young Harry Sargent attended. The house his family lived in for a while is in an adjoining street.

We read that one of Max's first jobs was in a fish and chip shop in the street at the bottom of my road, and Max's father 'sang for his beer' in a pub at the other end of the road. *Now there's a funny thing!*

I do hope you enjoy our New Blue Book. I am sure Max would be thrilled to know that there is still so much interest in his comedy and his life. Remember, no matter where he travelled, he always came home to the city and – to echo the words of our great friend and president, Roy Hudd – he died in his beloved Brighton in 1963.

EMPIRE
Supervisor
Manager
PRINCE LITTLER
JOHN CHRISTIE
G. W. A. HOARE
BOOK BY 'PHONE: BOWES PARK 4801
6.30
TWICE NIGHTLY
MONDAY, APRIL 28th, 1952
8.40
OVERTURE
MARTYN & COOKE
The Juggler and her Clown
MARTIN CROSBIE & THELMA
The Voice of Ireland
MADAME TRUZZI and her PETS
One and Only
MAX MILLER
MAX MILLER
"The Pure Gold of the Music Hall"
Lionel Hale—Daily Mail.
10 REG SALMON & COMPANY
OBTAINABLE ONLY ON PARLOPHONE
12. "HUTCH" (Leslie A. Hutchinson)
Entertainer at the Piano
13. MAX MILLER
The Cheeky Chappie
Tea and Coffee served in the Auditorium on request
This Theatre is fully licensed.
Matinees—WEDNESDAY and THURSDAY at 2.30
The Coconut Grove
THE PLACE TO GO AFTER THE SHOW"
EXCELLENT CUISINE
CABARET
TWO DISTINCT PROGRAMMES
DANCING
WOOD GREEN
LONDON PALLADIUM
George Black's
APPLE-SAUCE!
A NEW REVUE SHOWERED WITH STARS!
6d.
PROGRAMME
EMPIRE
FINSBURY PARK
Programme
GOLDERS GREEN HIPPODROME
PROGRAMME
VARIETY
6.15
8.30
MAX MILLER
CLIFFORD STANTON
SPENCE & DAVIES
RESTAURANT
Max Miller
WHENEVER YOU LIKE
HIS EXCLUSIVE RECORDINGS
IN THE THEATRE MADE BY
"HIS MASTER'S VOICE"
during actual public performances
include
HOLBORN EMPIRE
FIRST HOUSE
SECOND HOUSE

"There'll Never Be Another!" has proven to be Max's most famous catchphrase over the years. So when a quarterly magazine was suggested soon after the Appreciation Society was formed, editor Jack Strutt knew there could only be one title . . .

There'll Never Be Another

The Max Miller Appreciation Society started life in Brighton in January 1999 and the honour of being the first person to join went to the late Peter Dulay, producer of the long-running ITV show "Candid Camera".

Roy Hudd, a big fan of Max, immediately took up our invitation to be the Society's first president, and Ken Dodd was "tickled" to become a patron.

We were fortunate to find that Max's pianist in the 1950s/60s, Clive Allen, still lived in Brighton, and he gave the Society great support and became our first vice-president. Together with Lis Solkhon, who had also been on the bill with Max at that time, Clive put on several shows for the Society.

He was followed as vice-president by the "Welsh Prince of Laughter", Wyn Calvin. Michael Aspel joined Ken as a patron, and other stars who have swelled our ranks at different times include Cyril Fletcher, Graham Stark, Ronnie Ronalde, Peter Blake, Michael Grade, Bruce Forsyth and Jonathan Ross. We have also enjoyed the support of many other talented and knowledgeable people with an interest in Max and the wonderful world of Variety.

The Society's magazine "There'll Never Be Another" first saw the light of day in May 1999 and has appeared quarterly ever since. During that time TNBA – as it soon became known by members – has explored every aspect of Max's life and career – from his early school days, his first comedy experience with Jack Sheppard's Entertainers on Brighton seafront, a ten-year film career, numerous recordings of both his live act and his saucy songs, a brief TV exposure in the late 1950s and, of course, 40 years on the Halls including three Royal Variety Show appearances.

TNBA has featured many rare variety bills and sheet music of most of his songs. Jack is always on the lookout for other examples and can be contacted by writing to him at 111, Brentwood Road, Brighton, BN1 7ET or telephoning 01273 500168.

HERE AM I
BROKEN HEARTED
Let's Have A Ride On Your
WHAT'S THE MATTER WITH THE GRAVY?
BERNIE READ
FREDDIE JOHNS
MAX MILLER
FOR OLD TIMES SAKE
MAX MILLER
AIN'T LOVE GRAND
LESLIE SARONY
MARY FROM THE DAIRY
Words by SAM KERN, MAX MILLER & JAMES WALSH
EVERYTHING HAPPENS TO
MAX MILLER
OH! MA, LEAVE THE DOOR AJAR
RED SANFORD
RTHUR LE CLERQ
MAX MILLER
B. FELDMAN & Co
ALWAYS THE SA
SWEET PAL
SONG WALTZ
JUST ANOTHER SALLY
(DOWN ANOTHER ALLEY)
FEATURED BY MAX MILLER
THE OLD OAK TREE

Max may have died in 1963, but thanks to the MMAS and people like the entertainer John Ripley, his humour lives on. John, who joined the Society in 2001, has created a tribute act to the great man himself. He sounds like him, looks like him - and makes people laugh just as the Cheeky Chappie did. So we asked John what it's like . . .

Being Max Today

Well, it all started when I was invited to entertain at a monthly get-together of the Appreciation Society – which used to meet then at a social club on Marine Parade in Brighton.

My performance appeared to go down quite well and soon, along with my pianist Theo Squire, I was invited to perform at the Society's annual dinner. Then I helped at the launch of the first Blue Book in a Brighton bookshop, and that's where I met Clive Allen, who had been Max's pianist for the last fifteen years of his life.

Clive told me some lovely stories about the man and the venues and the music hall characters of their day. Subsequently I had many telephone chats with him before, sadly, he died in 2003 at the age of 86.

One very interesting point that Clive told me was that in all the many years he had been with Max, never once did he hear him mention the name of John East, who wrote his biography in 1977.

Over the years I have been very fortunate to be asked to appear at some wonderful venues. The Grosvenor House and Dorchester Hotels on Park Lane in London were up there with the best. Then there were the Odeon in Leicester Square, the Metropole, Brighton, the Pavilion Theatre, Worthing and the Theatre Royals at Margate and Brighton. I also enjoy entertaining many active retirement associations and old folks' homes. They all love Max, of course!

As far as the Max Miller Appreciation Society is concerned, despite living in Gravesend I always try to make myself available to attend their meetings and functions, thus helping to keep the name of Max Miller in the public eye as long as we can.

Believe me, I've had a great time in my years with the Society and met up with some smashing people – long may it continue!

John can be contacted on (day) 01474 564507 or (evening) 01474 536305.

A mix of Maxes . . . clockwise from left: Peter Garrett, John Ripley, Peter Wentworth, Bob Eaton and Tony Scarrott.

Listen ! Listen !

Those of you who were fortunate enough to read the first Blue Book (Thanks by the way: part of Max's statue in Brighton is down to you – don't ask which part, though) you'll almost certainly notice that most of the jokes in that unique publication are repeated in this one.

Yes, including the one about the 'narrow mountain pass' madam! Many of us doubt whether Max ever told it – but then along comes someone to state emphatically that he *did*! And they heard him tell it, so . . .

Yes, all the old jokes are here, but then Max practically toured the world telling 'em, and no-one ever complained, did they? Well, not very often! Mention a chihuahua and people in the business will grin and say: "Max Miller !" Nudist using the telephone ? "Maxie!" "What's what ?" You've guessed it – our hero!

So no excuses for using all the old jokes, boys and girls, but, just to tickle your fancy – have you ever had your fancy (that's f-a-n-c-y) tickled, missus? – we've included a few 'new' jokes that we reckon the Cheeky Chappie might have paid half-a-crown for at the stage door . . .

'Ere!

What about the two old men sitting in the Pavilion Café. One turns to the other and says, "Do you remember when we used to chase the girls along the prom?"

The other replied, "Yes – I remember chasing 'em, but I can't remember for the life of me why."

Emergency Call down at Hove Police Station. "Hurry please, I want to report a burglar trapped in the bedroom of an old spinster."

"We'll be right round," said the policeman, "Who am I talking to?

"The burglar!"

You didn't know I was artistic, did you lady? Well, this beautiful girl came up to me – I was adjusting my easel in Preston Park at the time. She came up to me and said, "Can you paint me in the nude?"

"Certainly" I replied, "but I'll have to keep my socks on. I must have somewhere for the brushes."

"Excuse me, sir, the wife wants me to go shopping with her – may I have the afternoon off ?"

"Certainly not !"

"Thank you sir, I knew you'd understand."

MICHAEL ASPEL OBE

TV personality Michael Aspel has been a Max Miller fan since his South London childhood. As Patron of the Max Miller Appreciation Society, he talks exclusively here about one TV programme he would have liked to present . . .

Max Miller made his first film "The Good Companions" in 1933, the year I was born (it was also the year that Hitler came to power – so the news wasn't all good). Although I never saw Max give a live performance, I did once encounter him in the flesh. I was marching through the lounge of a Cardiff hotel in the early 1950s, when I spotted the great man stretched out in an armchair. He realised from the way that I skidded to a halt and gaped at him that I was a fan. He looked up, raised a hand and gave me a warm smile. Then he spoke, and the words he uttered will stay with me for the rest of my life: "Hello, son."

Max would have made a perfect subject for "This Is Your Life". His wife Kathleen could have told us how she persuaded him to change his name. The *Daily Mail*'s theatre critic could have recalled the show at the London Casino in 1947 that led him to anoint Max "The Pure Gold of the Music Hall". And Roy Hudd could have explained how he came to be the owner of Max's guitar.

Of course, television wasn't Max's natural habitat, but we always had a live audience and he would have spent the entire recording on his feet, playing to them.

So, sadly, no Big Red Book. But, hang on – here's a New Blue one! The Max Miller Appreciation Society has done it again. Let's raise a glass of bubbly (we'll even pay for it ourselves – something Max rarely did) to this latest collection in the name of our hero.

The Cheeky Chappie said,

"Now I'll tell you what I'm going to do. I'm going to tell you some stories and I want you to shout out the answers. When I tell some old jokes, I'm going to test your memory to see how far you can go back. And I want you to understand that the jokes I'm going to tell you were good enough for your grandfather to laugh at, and they're good enough for you. Now, I've got two books. I've got a white book and a blue book, and by that you can gather I've got two sorts of stories. I'm going to start on the white book first. Now shout the answers out..."

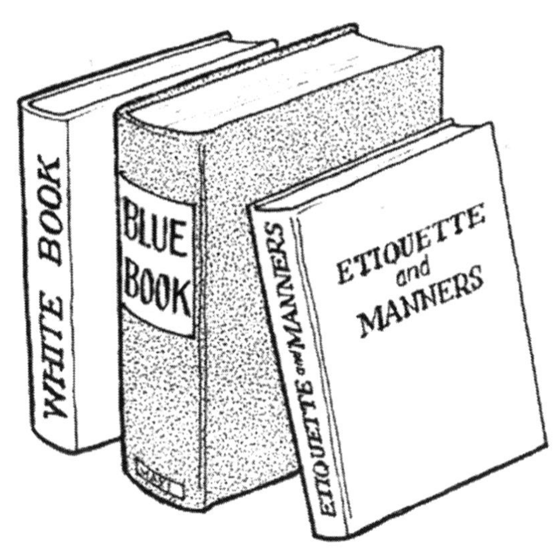

The Cheeky Chappie's books . . . "They don't make 'em any more, Duck!"

"Listen, listen, are you listening?"

Why did the chicken cross the road? To get to the other side? I'm going back further than that. These are old jokes. It says in the white book, 'Why did the chicken cross the road? For some foul reason.'

You heard about the Yorkshire man who came to London and couldn't get some Yorkshire pudding. He went home and battered himself to death.

He said, "I'm a travelling salesman."
I said, "Where're your bags?"
He said, "I got one under each eye."

As I always say, the only right way to get on in life is to start at the bottom and work your way up. Unless, of course, you're a parachutist.

I'd tell you the story of the red-hot poker, only I don't think you'd grasp it.

The Cheeky Chappie said, "It says in the white book, listen!"

Cold chicken

I bought a car the other day, a used car, and I don't know what it was used for. So I said to the fellow, "What is it?"

He said, "It's a coupé."

I said, "That's what they keep birds in."

He said, "That's right." So he went to the back of the car and he opened it and he brought out a chicken.

He said, "Will you stay for lunch?"

I said, "Yes, I'll stay."

He took all the feathers off the chicken and put it in the oven and closed the door. He said, "When we come back, we'll have that."

So we came back and, he opened the door, and when he opened the oven door the chicken said, "Listen, either put my feathers back or light the gas. It's bloody cold in here."

The grass is greener

I looked out of the window this morning and saw a man, eating grass in the front garden.

I said, "What are you doing?"

He said, "I'm starving."

I said, "When you're finished there, go round the back – the grass is longer."

Piccadilly

There's a little mouse walking along the pavement in Piccadilly and a woman frightened it and it stepped off the kerb and got knocked down by a bus and picked itself up and went across the road into a music shop and said to the man behind the counter, "Do you sell mouse organs?"

And the man said, "That's funny. That's funny you should say that. We had a little mouse in here yesterday and she wanted mouse organs."

And the little mouse said, "I know who that was. That was our-Monica."

A tramp stopped a woman and said, "I haven't eaten for five days."

"Well, my good man," she said, "you'll have to force yourself."

Listen – this old lady – she left all her money to a brothel – she thought it was a soup kitchen.

Do you know the difference between an old man, young man and a worm? There's no difference, the birds get them all.

The Cheeky Chappie said, "You can't expect too much from the white book. THIS is the book. This is where we all get pinched. I don't care. I'll go. I've been there before. I have. I won't walk. I make them get the barrow out. I'm on the BLUE BOOK now."

Have you heard about the girl of eighteen who swallowed a pin, but didn't feel the prick until she was twenty-one?

A girl joined the army as a man, a fellow was telling me.

I said, "I can't see that at all. She couldn't get away with that." I said, "How about when they all take a bath? Wouldn't they find out?"

He said, "But who'd tell?"

This girl invited me up to her flat for coffee and games. I said, "Don't bother with the coffee."

We arrived and she said, "I didn't work as a stiffener in a laundry for nothing."

"I must tell you. 'Ere let me tell you..."

A pal of mine, a master builder. He said to his little boy around Christmas time, "What would you like for Christmas?" So the boy said, "I'd like a baby brother."

The master builder said, "We couldn't finish the job on time." He said, "You can have a gun or a horse."

The boy said, "No, I don't want a gun or a horse, I want a baby brother."

The fellow said, "I told you, we can't finish the job on time."

The boy said, "Well, you could put more men on the job."

Now, listen!

A fellow I know was going away for a few days. He was going to Manchester. He didn't know where to stay. I said, " I can tell you where to stay and I told him, it's a nice hotel, the food's good and the beds are marvellous and the boss is a very nice chap and he doesn't charge you a penny. As a matter of fact at the end of the week he gives you a few quid to go home with."

He said, "Have you stayed there?"

I said, "No, but my sister has."

My young nephew, Roland was having a lesson in grammar and his teacher wrote down on the blackboard, "I didn't have no fun at the seaside."

She turned round and said, "Roland, how should I correct that?"

"Get a boy friend," he told her.

"'Ere's One!"

A rabbit's tale

A female rabbit – she was having a nibble – with a male rabbit. Eating grass, see? She got a bit coy, see. She said to the male rabbit, "Would you like a little family?"

The male rabbit said, "That won't take us long, did it?"

"Ma! – I've just learned how to multiply!"

Underground

I was on the tube the other day. It was rush hour and we were packed to suffocation. There I was, pressed against this beautiful blonde.

Me? No, I wouldn't! You're awful, you are!

Anyway, the train stopped and she said to me, "Is this Cockfosters?"

And I said, "No – it's Wood Green, and the name's Miller."

'Ere!

The Cheeky Chappie said, "A little monologue as spoken from the mouth."

There was an old cow from Huddersfield.
No milk would that old cow yield.
The reason why no milk she'd yield,
She didn't like her udders feeled.

Going nuts

I was walking through the forest the other day and I heard a cry in the distance like "oh, oh!" not very loud, not very loud, you know, "oh!" So I walked towards the cry and when I got there, there was a fellow standing under a tree, practically in the nude with a bag of nuts in his hand. So I said, "Why are you crying?"

He said, "Well, you hear it over the radio all the time. They are appealing for this, appealing for that. Give your old clothes to people who want them." He said, "Well I've done that."

"I can see that," I said, "Give your money to the hospital."

He said, "I've done that."

I said, "I don't know why you're crying."

He said, "Look what it says on that tree behind me. Give your nuts to the squirrels."

The Girls Who Do!

The Girls Who Do!

The Cheeky Chappie said, "Listen, Listen!"

I like the girls who do,
I like the girls who don't,
I hate the girl who says she will
And then she says she won't.
But the girl I like the best of all
And I think you'll say I'm right,
Is the girl who says she never does
But she looks as though she... ***'Ere!***

Stormy weather

I took this girl home for a spot of pleasure. Didn't know I was kinky, did you? I told her to put her leather boots on, and got her to sit on the top of the chest of drawers.

She said, "What now?"

I said, "Put your arm out and turn the light on and off and, after that, pour that basin of water over your head."

She got that bothered and she said, "When are we going to get down to a bit of the other?"

I said, "What – in this weather?"

"'Ere, what's the difference? I'll ask you a question, and see if you can answer it."

What's the difference between a girl getting out of a car and a rude joke? I bet you don't know... I'll tell you. Sometimes you see it and sometimes you don't.

Met a girl the other day. I said, "You've got a nice figure," and she replied, "Yes, and I don't want you to spoil it."

A change from the wife – she weighs twenty stone – that tells you what a lot I have to get through.

When roses are red,
They're ready for plucking.
When a girl is sixteen,
She's ready for... ***'Ere!***

She's a girl who's just built to my liking.
A wonderful figure has Nellie...
Two rosy lips and very broad hips
And a nice little mole on her shoulder.

"Now there's a funny thing"

I said to a girl friend, "This is funny. Every time I call round to your house your husband's out." I said, "Where does he go?"

She said, "He goes round to your house."

Making a pass

I was walking along this narrow mountain pass, so narrow that nobody else could pass you, when I saw a beautiful blonde walking towards me. A beautiful blonde with not a stitch on, yes, not a stitch on, lady. Cor blimey, I didn't know whether to toss myself off or block her passage.

The Cheeky Chappie says, "You wicked lot, you're the type of people that give me a bad name!"

Once upon a time a thousand years ago there were four good girls – a thousand years ago, once upon a time. And in those days they would come to London and stop at the YWCA. Now they come to London and stop at nothing.

Pleasant Dreams!

I remember I was staying in a small town, a mining town, and I couldn't find digs and I went round looking for rooms and I knocked on a door and a beautiful woman came to the door and she said, "Yes?"

And I said, "Wait a minute, I haven't asked you yet."

She said, "Do you want food?"

I said, "Why, is there anything else?" I said, "Could you put me up for the night?"

She said, "I'm full up."

I said, "But surely you could squeeze me in a back room, couldn't you?"

She said, "I could, but I haven't got time now."

So I said, "How much do you charge?"

She said, "Thirty shillings all in and I don't want any children."

I said, "I'm not married, I've always been round shouldered."

She said, "The best I can do for you is, you can sleep with baby if you like and it'll cost you a pound."

I said, "No, I'm not having that. I can walk about and get wet through."

She said, "Would you sleep in the front room on the couch?"

"Yes, I'll do that." So I went to sleep in the front room on the couch and in the early morning a beautiful blonde walked in with a cup of tea.

I said, "Who are you?"

She said, "I'm baby. Who are you?"

I said, "I'm the mug that slept on the couch."

"I've been to a wedding – the girlfriend's."
"Did you give her away?"
"No, I never said a word."

"All clever stuff, no rubbish!"

I saw a girl who was proud of her figure. Just to make conversation I asked her, "What would you do if a chap criticised your figure?"
"Well," she said, "I wouldn't hold it against him."

A girl said to me, she said, "Maxie, why do men get up in the early hours of the morning?"
I said, "What do you mean, in the middle of the night?"
She said, "Yes."
I said, "Well, ten per cent get up to go to the kitchen to get something to eat. And twenty per cent get up because they want to go out. And the other seventy per cent get up to go home. That's all I can think of."

She said, "Wasn't it funny how we met?"
He said, "I thought you smiled at me when you sat down."
She said, "Smiled? I nearly laughed outright."
He said, "Why?" She said, "You look like a boy who wouldn't say boo to a goose."
He said, "I don't speak to birds at all as a rule."

The Cheeky Chappie said, "They don't make 'em any more, duck!"

"As I always say, lady ..."

If a fast girl uses too much lipstick, it will be on every man's lips.

Some dew!

A girl was wearing a v-necked sweater and I said to her,
"What does the V stand for – Victory?"
She said, "No, virgin."
I said, "I bet it's a very old sweater."

Dew respect

Listen! I was going home the other morning, at daybreak – I wouldn't venture out at night. As I was going along a country road, I saw a young lady. She was coming towards me. When she got up right near me, I looked at her and said, "Can I see you home?"

She said, "No, I'm going the other way."

I said, "I can turn round."

So I turned round, see, and we started to walk in the middle of the road. I said, "Let's get up on the path."

So we got up on the path and it was all grass on the path, so I bent down and felt the grass and said, "Some dew," and she said, "Some don't – good morning."

Game girls

She was one of these clever girls, you know the type I mean, and she had a very nice figure. I said, "You have a very nice figure."

She said, "What do you want to do, spoil it?"

Matter of fact she had everything. The trouble was she had it all in one place. I said, "I got something for you."

She said, "What you've got for me I can do without." She said, "Besides, I'm not that kind of a girl."

I said, "What makes you think that I'm that kind of a man?"

She said, "It's your eyes. They are the same colour as your gags." She said, "Will you come up to the flat for coffee and games?"

I said, "I'll come up but don't bother with the coffee. Not straight away." So I went up. She had a marvellous flat, two beautiful armchairs. We didn't bother with those and she had a lovely bearskin in front of the fire. I was glad the fire was on! So was she I think. No, well, it was raining outside and there are only two things you can do when it's raining and I don't play cards! So she got the draughts out and we started to play draughts and I was doing all right until she got me in a corner and crowned me. I said, "How long is this game going to take?"

She said, "I don't know Maxie. How long can you stay?"

I said, "Well I can't stay long, a couple of days at the most."

So I kissed her good-night the following morning and at the door she said, "Aren't you shy, you're a shy boy, aren't you?" She said, "Don't you believe in free love?"

I said, "No I don't." I don't think she did, either. I was a pound short when I got home.

Ni-ice girls

I went skating the other week with a young lady on ice and we'd been going around for quite a while and she kept on falling down. I said, "Have you hurt yourself?"

She said, "No, I'm sorry to spoil your fun."

I said, "you're not spoiling my fun. It'll keep on ice."

No holds barred

By the way, how did a poor struggling girl get a fur coat? She stopped struggling.

Experienced girls

The other day I went for a drive in my car and I met a young lady. She was walking in the middle of the road, beautifully dressed, so I stopped the car and raised my hat. The wife allows me to do that. I said, "Can I give you a lift?"

She said, "No, thanks. I'm just walking back from one."

I said, "Can I drive you home? I like driving experienced girls home."

She said, "I'm not experienced."

I said, "You're not home yet."

We were going along very nicely together then all of a sudden she said, "Can you drive with one hand?"

I said, "No, but I can stop." So we stopped. We went into a hotel. I said, "What would you like?"

She said, "I'll have a banana split."

I said, "I don't think they can do it."

She said, "All right, I'll have a banana sundae."

I said, "You can't get a banana sundae. You might get a pancake Tuesday or a Sheffield Wednesday." I said, "Why don't you have a whisky soda?"

She said, "Drink takes the coat off your stomach."

I said, "In that case my stomach must be walking about in shirt sleeves." I said, "Will you marry me or go and enjoy yourself?"

She said, "What do you do for a living?"

I said, "I'm a railway inspector."

She said, "Why should I marry you because you're a railway inspector?"

I said, "You can travel all over my system for nothing."

Smart girls

It's not very easy being a lady's accountant. They say figures can't lie, but I know two figures that can't even stand up.

You'd be surprised what some girls do say to me. A girl came up to me the other day and said, "Max, have you got it?" I said, "I've got all there is. You can't have any more and that's it."

And another girl came up to me and said, "Aren't you ugly?" I said, "I can't help my looks." And she said, "No, but you can stay indoors."

I went to a dance last night and I said to the girl, "That's a smart dress you're wearing." She said, "Yes, all the smart girls are buying them now." I said, "That's where you're wrong. Smart girls don't buy anything." Well she hit me in the mouth and I closed up like a bank holiday.

She was beautifully dressed this girl, beautifully dressed. I said, "You must spend all your money on clothes." She said, "Where would a girl be without her clothes?" I said, "You tell me, I'll be there."

Well, this blonde obviously took a fancy to me. She said she worked in a chemist's shop until she let the pharm-a-see. Now she's got a job in a photographer's shop. I said, "You look well developed."

Wild girls

As I always say, lady, some girls are like flowers. They grow wild in the woods.

Oh, I must tell you this one. Listen! I remember when I went to a dance, I said to a young lady, "Can I see you home?"

She said, "I don't allow boys to take me home."

I said, "Why not?"

She said, "Last night I let Johnny Smith take me home."

I said, "You should be proud that he took you home, because his father, like myself, is a self-made man, and you can imagine the struggle he had."

She said, "Can you imagine the struggle *I* had!"

'Ere, I got one...

She said, "Why don't you behave yourself like your forefathers?"

I said, "Did I have four fathers?"

She said, "Everybody had forefathers."

I said, "If I did, three of them never came home."

Dora went swimming the other day and sat on a broken bottle on the beach. She went to the doctor who said, "Where is the injury?"

"Well, doctor," said Dora. "I'll show you if you promise not to look."

Loose girls

Lure them, love them and lose them, that's my motto, and when I lose a girl she stays lost and when I leave them they stay left. And when I've left them, they're not right anymore.

That reminds me of the chorus girl who married a rich old invalid. She promised to take him for better or worse. She really took him for worse, but he got better.

A pal of mine married a typist. They get along just the same as before. When he dictates to her, she takes him down.

Then there was this skipper of this cargo boat who got on well with the girls. Naturally, he knew every hold.

Dead right!

I said to a girl, "Are you familiar with Shakespeare?"

She said, "Yes, as a matter of fact I had dinner with him last night."

I said, "Don't be a mug, he's been dead a hundred years."

She said, "I thought he was quiet."

Girls who don't

I met a girl at a bus stop and she said, "Will you marry me? I'm different from other girls?"

And I said, "If you are too different, I'll have to consider it." I said, "Would you like to go for a drive?"

She said, "No thanks, I'm too tired, I'd sooner walk." Well anyway she got into the car and I noticed she was wearing a big bangle on her wrist. So I said, "What's that?"

She said, "It's a suppressor."

I said, "I've got one of those on the car, it stops interference."

She said, "That's why I'm wearing it."

Pet's corner

This girl had a little dog and it was very hairy. So she went to the chemist and said, "Do you have anything for removing superfluous hair?"

He said, "Yes, I've got my own prescription. You just rub it on your legs and ten minutes later the hair will be gone."

"Oh," she said, "It isn't for my legs, it's for my little Chihuahua."

He said, "In that case, **don't ride your bike for a fortnight!**"

The Cheeky Chappie said, "Boys will be boys, otherwise you girls wouldn't have any fun!"

Max's Missus

Ready and waiting

The Cheeky Chappie said, "My wife...

Listen, listen!"

Between you and me, my wife's the ugliest woman in the world. I'd rather take her with me than kiss her goodbye. But we never row, the wife and I. And you know why? Because I help her with everything. Yesterday I did the washing with her, today I did the ironing with her, tomorrow I'm going to do the cooking with her, then on Saturday I'm going to wipe the floor with her.

Before I was married, I was courting my wife for ten years. Then I went round to see her father and I looked straight at him. He said, "Hello." I said, "Hello." He said, "What do you want?"

I said, "I've been courting your daughter for ten years."

He said, "So what?"

I said, "I want to marry her."

He said, "I thought you wanted a pension."

"Are you listening?"

He said, "If you marry my daughter, I'll give you three acres and a cow."

You're quite right, quite right – I'm still waiting for the three acres.

I'd only been married a week, a week, when I found the wife's nightdress on the bed with fur round the bottom. I said, "What's the fur round the bottom for?"

She said, "My mother told me to keep my neck warm."

When we were on our honeymoon, a man came running past the bedroom door. So the next morning I said to him, "What's the idea? Monday night you ran past the bedroom door, Tuesday night you ran past and Wednesday night you ran past, then Thursday you skipped past."

He said, "Well, the doctor gave me some medicine and told me to take it three nights running and the fourth night skip it."

I took the wife out the other week on the back of my motorbike. And can she talk? She can never stop talking. Yap, yap, yap all the time. And we were going along. I was doing 50 miles an hour and I could still hear her talking; 60 miles an hour she was still talking; at 70 miles an hour she was driving me mad. I looked through the glass and saw a police car following me. I said hello, he's chasing me, so I was away doing 80 miles an hour when, all of a sudden, he stopped me and said, "Listen, I'm not going to pinch you for speeding, but I want to tell you your wife has fallen off about two miles back."

I said, "Thank God for that. I thought I had gone stone cold deaf."

The Cheeky Chappie said,

"Ain't love grand?"

I must be the best husband in the world. I keep going home! I said to the wife, I said, "Do you believe it when I say I love you?"

"She said, "I do."

I said, "Do you believe me when I say I worship the very ground you walk on?"

"She said, "I do."

I said, "Do you believe me when I say I would die for you?"

"She said, "I do."

I said, "Then you must be raving mad."

Not bad is it?

My wife said to me the other day, "From now on I'm going to wear the trousers."

I said, "That's all right with me." Can you imagine a woman going to bed hanging them behind the door? Why, she'd be getting up in the middle of the night stealing her own money!

My wife's always complaining she hasn't any clothes to wear. It takes her two hours to put them on when we're going out. So I thought I'd teach her a lesson. I went home one night and I said, "I got two tickets for the theatre."

She said, "Good, I'll go upstairs and get ready."

I said, "I should, they're for tomorrow night!"

"As I always say, lady..."

I have the best wife in England, although I say it myself. The other one's in Africa. She went to the pictures yesterday and when she came home, she told me she changed her seat fourteen times. I said, "Were you molested?"

She said, "Yes, eventually."

She said, "I get very lonely when you're away. Only last week a burglar broke in.

I said, "Did he get anything?"

She said, "Yes, I thought it was you." She said, "I half killed him."

That's covered that one up, hasn't it?

With a little bit of luck

Well, when I got home, I had a few words with the wife. This is straight; I mean this. Well, married people do, they argue, there's no doubt about it. You've got to; otherwise it wouldn't be married life. She said to me, "Who was that blonde I saw you with last week?"

I said, "I don't really know who she is but she was going to the dogs and I was showing her the way."

She said, "Listen, Miller, no woman's going to upset my married life. We've been married far too long."

I said, "I wouldn't say that."

She said, "No, but you think it."

She got a mouthful!

But she's not a bad woman really. I don't know what I'd do without her... if I had the chance. She'd give anything away – good-natured. Trouble is, when she opens her mouth, she gives *herself* away. She's got a mouth, I'm not kidding. It's like the black hole of Calcutta. She fell off her bike the other day, just outside the house and I went to pick her up and I thought she'd hurt herself as she was laughing. Got the handlebars in her mouth.

Friends and neighbours

The fellow next-door, he hates the sight of me. He said to my wife, "I saw your husband this morning. I saw him on the beach with a blonde in his arms."

She said, "Well, what do you expect him to have at his age, a bucket and spade?"

I spend half my life getting into trouble and half my life getting out.

And the woman next-door, oh dear, oh dear, I can't get on with her at all. She's very nosey. Oh, she is nosey. She said, "I heard you rowing again last night." She said, "If I had married you, I'd have given you poison."

I said, "If I was married to you, I would have taken it and all, don't bother."

The Cheeky Chappie said, "I got home late last night"

I got home late last night. Well, you know how it is lady! You look as if you do! No, 'ere, listen! I'd had a drop y'see and I could hear this little angel voice saying, "Pretty buttercup" over and over again. Lovely it was. And when I got upstairs, I told my wife, see, and she said, "That wasn't an angel, that was me saying: bring the bucket up!"

I took the wife to Bournemouth one week. The hotel manager said to me, "We're full up."

I said, "Surely you can put us in somewhere?"

He said, "Well, you can have the bridal suite, if you like."

I said, "The bridal suite? We've been married for forty years."

He said, "You can have the ballroom, but you don't have to dance."

I've just come back from my holiday. I always have a wonderful time when I go on my holidays, because I haven't got one of those wives who say, "Where have you been? How much have you spent? Who have you been with?"

She doesn't say that. She comes with me.

Apple sauce

You'll like this. I took her to a cabaret one night and we sat down and the waitress said, "Do you want food?" And I said, "Is there anything else?"

She said, "There's à la carte roast beef Max Miller."

I said, "Why do you call it à la carte roast beef Max Miller?"

She said, "It's a bit near the knuckle."

Now then, not bad is it? Well, after we'd eaten, the manager gave me the bill – four pounds ten. I said, "This is wrong, four pounds ten; it should only be two pounds." I said, "What's the two pounds ten for?"

He said, "That's for the use of the cruet."

I said, "I never used the cruet."

He said, "It was there if you wanted to." So I gave him two pounds. He said, "What about the other two pounds ten?"

I said, "That's for kissing my wife."

He said, "I never kissed your wife."

I said, "She was there if you wanted to."

Haw, Haw!

The wife got up very annoyed and she walked out. She was annoyed, just because I questioned the bill, that's all. So I said, "Goodbye, mother of three."

She said, "Goodbye, father of two."

"Now there's a funny thing, ladies and gentlemen; this is a funny thing."

What bust?

She said, "I'm going out tomorrow and I want you to do all the washing."
So I said, "All right." So I got all the clothes out and I put them in the washing machine and when I took them out, her brassiere was all in holes. So I went to a shop and I said to the girl, I said, "I want a brassiere."

She said, "What bust?"

I said, "I don't know, I think it wore out."

She said, "No, I mean what size?"

I said, "Fourteen."

She said, "There isn't such a size."

I said, "There must be, I take a seven bowler hat and that fits one of them."

"Now this is a funny thing. I went home the other night. Now there's a funny thing!"

I went home the other night and the wife had got two black eyes. I said, "Where did you get the black eyes?"

She said, "The lodger gave them to me."

I said, "Where's the lodger?"

She said, "Upstairs."

I shouted up and said, "Charlie, did you give my wife two black eyes?"

He said, "Yes."

I said, "What for?"

He said, "I found out she was unfaithful to us."

Dancing partner

Now my wife ... She weighs twenty-eight stone. It's too much; I know. You don't have to tell me. She goes dancing to get her weight down, but I don't think it makes any difference. She's got the advantage of thin girls when she goes dancing. She doesn't have to shimmy like the slim girls, she just walks quick and stops suddenly and lets nature takes its course.

The missus said to me yesterday, "Every time you see a pretty girl, you forget you are married."
"No," I told her, "I remember."

The Cheeky Chappie said, "Can you imagine that, lady? How's your memory gal?"

I went in the back way through the kitchen, through the dining room to the drawing room and there's a fellow there – not a stitch on. Can you imagine that, lady? How's your memory girl? He hasn't got a stitch on. I called the wife in. I said, "Who's this?"

She said, "Don't lose your temper, Miller. Don't go raving mad."

I said, "I'm only asking a fair question."

She said, "He's a nudist and he's come in to use the phone."

"There's a clever one from the wife, eh?"

Oh yes! She knows her onions

I went home the other night and I caught the wife in the front room sitting on a white horse in the nude. I said, "Who are you supposed to be?"

She said, "I'm Lady Godiva."

I said, "Lady Godiva was a great tipster – she's the greatest tipster. She put everything she had on a horse."

The wife said, "What do you think I'm doing?"

The following night I went home and I caught the wife again. I caught her in the arms of the milkman. I said, "This can't be right, it's the coalman we owe the money to."

The Cheeky Chappie says, "It's all good stuff, lady."

I'm the happiest man in the world. I should be. I've got a life and a wife and they're both working. Only yesterday I said to the wife, "Is it true that absence makes the heart grow fonder?"

She said, "Go away for a long time and I'll write and let you know."

She said she's going to divorce me because of my flat feet. She must have seen me putting them in the wrong flat.

Get off my foot!

Though I say it myself, the wife's got the biggest feet in the world. She wasn't feeling very well the other day. She said to the doctor, "I've got one foot in the grave."

He said, "You don't have to worry. You won't get both in."

Now isn't it funny,
I'm built on the small side,
The wife's built on the big side
Its always my dread that I'll fall out of bed,
That's why I sleep on the wall side.

The Cheeky Chappie said, "Well ... What if I am, love?"

My wife, she weighs twenty stone. What I go through! On our wedding night she woke me up and started shouting, "Here, here." And I started shouting, "Where, where?"

It's funny how I met my wife. She cocked one eye at me and I cocked one eye at her, and there we stood both of us cockeyed.

My wife talks through her nose. My pal said, "What's wrong with her mouth?" I said, "It's worn out!"

Bare-faced cheek ...

The wife was taking a bath the other morning and a fellow started to clean the window. He was looking through the window and she jumped out of the bath and she stood there as she came into the world. And he looked at her and he said, "What are you staring at? Haven't you seen a window cleaner before?"

Tit bits

I went home the other night and the wife was crying. I said, "What are you crying for?"

She said, "I'm homesick."

I said, "This *is* your home."

She said, "I know – I'm sick of it."

I've been married twice, so I know. I know what it's all about. I should do. I married my first wife by candlelight. It only lasted a wick.

I met my second wife in a beautiful garden, in an old English garden, and there she was hanging out the washing on a fruit tree. I never knew she had so many pears.

I phoned the wife from the office. I said, "I may be late in tonight. I have a fair bit to do at the office!"

I bought her a violin last week to give her chin a rest.

A married man must love his wife, but a navvy can have his pick.

"Listen, listen, listen! Are you listening?"

They took the vanity from the peacock,
The cunning from the fox,
The brains from a jackass,
The jawbone from an ox,
The venom from the viper,
The stinger from the bee,
Put them all in my old woman,
And bunged her on to me.

I call my wife carefree. She doesn't care, so long as everything's free. She said to me, "You've never done a good turn in your life for anyone."

I said, "I don't know. I once did a good turn for a bad girl. I think I was very foolish, because I don't think she'd do a good turn for me any more."

Don't get me wrong

Although I talk a lot about my wife, it might surprise you, ladies and gentlemen, to know that we're very happily married. We've only had one row and that was on our wedding night – and it's lasted up till now.

NOW FOR SOME BANTER and BATTER . . .

The moment John Henty walked into Bardsley's Fish and Chips restaurant in Baker Street, Brighton, he knew that this was the place for the Max Miller Appreciation Society to celebrate its hero with a permanent display of Miller memorabilia.

Bardsley's boss, Roy Brown, is known locally as the "Cheeky Chippy", and customers from all over the world flock to the unpretentious restaurant for his friendly banter and unbeatable batter.

The Max Miller room features one of Max's outrageous stage suits, early photographs of the artist, music hall posters and a superb pub sign which was rescued from a builder's skip in South London by a Society member.

"I saw Max a few times when he appeared at the Hippodrome in Brighton" Roy recalls. "This tribute is our way of thanking him for the laughs!"

Bardsley's is still owned by the direct descendants of Ben Bardsley, who moved to Brighton from Lancashire during the Great Depression in 1926. He opened his original shop in Upper Russell Street and for many years this shop supported all subsequent generations of the family.

Today, the Baker Street restaurant is keeping the family tradition alive and has acquired a reputation for quality and friendly service. It is open Tuesday to Saturday 11.30-2.30 and 4-8.30. It is fully licensed. Telephone: (01273) 681256. It is always best to book.

PRINCE OF WALES
2.30
AUGUST 13th
6.30
VARIETY
MAX MILLER
EMP
6.30
MAX
MIKE & BERNIE WINTERS
TESSA SMALLPAGE
ROY STEVENS
don't GET ME WRO
FRIED FISH SHOP & RESTAUR
BARDSLEY'S Baker Street
THE ORIGINAL
THE MAX MILLER
NAT GONELL
GEORGIA ON MY MIND
EL
GRANADAS
MAX MILLER
ASKING FOR TROUBLE
BROKEN HEARTED
MAX MILLER
MAX MILLER
AT THE BATHING PARADE

10 CHEEKY YEARS OF
BLUE BOOK
MAX MILLER
Community Exhibitions
Listen, L
IT STAND UP FOR MAX
starring
EORGE
MELLY
BRIGHTON'S AWARD WINNI
TERRY GAROGHA
ADAM FAITH
MATT LUCAS
DES LYNAM
The Crazy World Of
ARTHUR BROWN
DON "Rosie" PARTRIDG
BERTIE PEARCE
& MISS ANGEL EYES
CHRIS GREEN as IDA BARR
EDINBURGH SENSATION 2002
THE KOMEDIA'S TOP DUO
DYBALL & KERR
urprise celeb from Brighton's WALK OF FAM
Variety show to raise funds for a permanent statue
remember Brighton's Cheeky Chappie, MAX MILLER
Sunday 24 November 7.45
SOUVENIR PROGRAMME
www.
maxmiller.org

CELEBRATING MAX
MAX MILLER
COMEDIAN AND FILM STAR

ROCK OF AGES

It is safe to say that the Max Miller Appreciation Society's annual garden party in August has become one of the top social events in the city's colourful and often flamboyant diary.

Held at the Pavilion Gardens Café, celebrity guests from the world of showbusiness mix happily with local V.I.P.s, different charities benefit each year and everyone enjoys the delicious food provided by David Sewell and his cheery team.

David's grandfather, Herbert Tennent, opened his first Brighton café to the west of the Palace Pier in the late 1920s. He moved to the Pavilion Gardens, close by the Royal Pavilion, in the early stages of the war and then in 1950, the present art deco style building was established in the current location and remains in use today.

As writer Peter Oakes confirmed in QueenSpark Books 2011 publication *Teatime Tales,* "It is one of the chief pleasures of being in Brighton, particularly at the height of summer, to spend time idling at the Pavilion Gardens Café. The ritual of queuing for tea and rock cakes and negotiating the best table, even in the midst of whirling children and dive-bombing pigeons, is reassuring, comfortable and quintessentially English."

To that David added - in the 70th year of trading - "This continuity and longevity enables regulars to feel like friends, and we are told this is one of the café's unique selling points and the reason our customers keep coming back for more. Or could it be the rock cakes, still baked to Herbert's recipe?"

Whatever the reason, for anyone visiting Max's statue close by, a Bert rock cake and cup of tea is the perfect way to toast the Cheeky Chappie!

"Listen, Listen!"

Girls, look after your figure
Or you'll get left on the shelf.
If you've a small figure,
Your chances are bigger.
Now figure it out for yourself.

They say laugh and grow fat, but I don't believe it. Every girl should have a slim figure in the ballroom and a fat one in the bank. I can help you to reduce both. Diet and exercise, that's what does it. I can change you from outsize to shop size before you know where you are. No chocolates, no pastries, no suet puddings, nothing, so what you pay for my advice you save on food.

It's quite true a woman has to starve herself in order to wear the fashionable gown, and her husband's got to starve himself to pay for it.

No woman likes to get stout unless she gets it in the bottle.

The Cheeky Chappie said, "I look nice now duck, don't I?"

I look better since I came back off my cruise, don't I? No, I was poorly… I was… I was dying. I look nice now duck. Don't I? I feel better too. I liked it. It was nice. I'm going again next year. I want to go again every year, because I had a cabin to myself, all to myself and next to me there was an old maid; she had a cabin to herself too. So I was all right, wasn't I? What? What? No, no. Me, I don't, I don't. No, honest I don't. I don't. Well, when I… look!

And one night, this old maid started screaming and bawling and banging on her door. She was making a terrible noise and the purser came along and said, "What's going on in here?"

She said, "There are two men in my room."

He said, "What do you want me to do?"

She said, "Sling one of them out."

So he slung me … *'Ere, Listen!*

A fellow walked into a tailor's and a woman said, "What do you want? Come this way."

He said, "I want to be measured for a suit."

So she took him in a back room. She measured him up, 34 chest, 32 waist, arms 33, 34. She measured the trousers, outside 33, inside 32. She said, "I'm not sure of that inside. I'd like to do that again." So she measured him inside again, 32. She said, "Is there anything else you want?"

He said, "I'd like a cap but really I'd like to be measured for another pair of trousers."

Let's all have a charabanc ride

Listen! Twenty women in a hospital, you see, and they were in a maternity ward. And the doctor was walking around one morning and he said to the first woman in the first bed, "When are you expecting your baby?" And she said, "On the 21st of November." And he went to the woman in the next bed and she said, "On the 21st of November." And he went right through and he got to the end and there was a woman fast asleep. He didn't want to wake her up, so he said to the woman in the other bed, "When's she expecting her baby?" And she said, "I can't tell you, because she didn't come with us on our charabanc trip."

All stitched up

I was looking for digs, and this woman opened the door.

"Yes?" she said, and I hadn't asked her. She said, "It'll be two pounds, all in, and I don't want children." She said, "I want what I want when I want it."

I said, "You'll get what I've got when I've got it."

She asked me to mind her baby that night. Did it howl! Gave it a dose of gin; got it to sleep, all right. When she got home, she said, "My! you are good with kids."

"No," I replied, "I can't bear them." She'd got eight kids. Caught her one night stitching up her husband's pyjamas.

"What's that for, girl?"

"Well, a stitch in time saves nine!"

Of course, I used to be a fortune-teller, and I remember a lady came to me one day and she said, "Mr Miller;" – called me Mr Miller, she wasn't forward. She said, "Can you find my husband for me?"

I said, "I'm a fortune-teller not a bloodhound."

I saw a lady standing on a soapbox addressing a crowd and she said, "Last night I was in the arms of the devil. Tonight I'm in the hands of an angel." And a drunken sailor said, "How are you fixed for tomorrow night?"

"Miller's the name, lady"

I just got back from my holidays. I went to Margate for the weekend. I spent two days looking for rooms. I knocked on the door and a dear old lady came to the door, so I said, "Could you accommodate me?"

She said, "I'm awfully sorry, I'm full up."

I said, "But surely you could squeeze me in a little back room, couldn't you?"

She said, "I could but I haven't got time now." Anyway she showed me the drawing room and when we got inside, she put the gramophone on. Of course, I rumbled straight away. She said, "Do you know There's a Rainbow Round My Shoulder?"

I said, "There's a tide mark round your neck."

Then she showed me the bedroom right at the top of the house overlooking the sea. She said, "This is the most expensive room in the house, £4.10.0 a minute."

A slanted roof, I couldn't stand up straight. I was on my knees all day. Then she showed me the kitchenette. You know what a kitchenette is, that's the patch between the sink and the tin of tomatoes.

I said, "Its cold in here, why don't you light the fire?"

She said, "The walls are so thin that, every time I light the fire the lady next door cooks her dinner."

"Whether you're rich or whether you're poor, it's nice to be rich. And whether you're married or whether you're single, it's nice anyway."

Last Train to Brighton

"I'm not strong, I'm not strong!"

Got my own studio in Brighton, lady. A woman came to the door at seven-thirty one morning. She said, "Max, I want you to paint a snake on my knee." I went dead white, honestly; no, well, I'm not strong, I'm not strong. So listen, I jumped out of bed, see – *listen a minute!*

I started painting a snake, just above her knee, that's where I started. But I had to chuck it in. She smacked me in the face. I didn't know a snake was that long. Well, how long is an ordinary snake?

Flight of fancy

There were three storks, mother stork, father stork and baby stork. Now mother stork flew over to Manchester and she delivered twins. Now father stork, he flew over to Birmingham and he delivered triplets. Now baby stork flew over to Brighton and put the wind up two barmaids.

The Cheeky Chappie said . . .

I was in Spain four year ago and in Spain all the girls wear little knives in the top of their stockings. I found that out. So I said to myself, I'll find out exactly what the idea is, so I said, "What's the idea of wearing a knife at the top of the stocking?"

She said, "That's to defend my honour."

I said, "What, a little tiny knife like that?" I said, "If you were in Brighton, you'd want a set of carvers!"

The Cheeky Chappie said "I used to be a swimming instructor myself in Brighton."

I used to take the girls out to teach them to swim, as they couldn't swim. If they could swim, I wouldn't go out with them. I've got no time to waste. And I remember the time, many years ago, middle of July, I took a young lady out. She couldn't swim. I went out three miles with her. I don't mess about on the shore. And when I got right out, I said to this beautiful woman, "Now what would you like to do?"

She said, "I'd like to do the breast stroke to start with."

I said, "Go on, I'll stand and watch you." So I stood on my stilts and she did the breaststroke. Then she said, "Now I think I'll turn over." And as she turned over, and may sand get in my eyes if I tell a lie, as she turned over I slipped my hand underneath her to hold her up, otherwise she'd go down. And I'm entitled to do that, because I'm a swimming instructor, you see.

I got my hand underneath, she's lying on her back on top of the water, her head will be about there, her feet there, my hand will be about . . . about *there*. No, shut up, shut up! No, well, I've lost me place now. Listen, listen! And all of a sudden she gave a scream, not a very loud scream. She went ooh! ooh! twice. I didn't hear her the first time; I was creeping up on her.

I said, "What are you screaming for?"

She said, "A shrimp's bitten me."

I said, "Don't be a mug, it's me." I said, "You want confidence."

She said, "You want handcuffs!"

Now listen!

The following day I took her sister out. It's according to their age how far I go out. She was thirty-five, her sister. I went out seven miles with her. And when I got out seven miles, I looked at this beautiful woman, thirty-five just going grey, on the turn she was. She started to cry.

I said, "What are you crying for? Have you done anything wrong?"

She said, "No."

I said, "Why haven't you?" Thirty-five.

She said, "I got the cramp." It's a shocking thing to get the cramp seven miles out in the water. It's all right in the bedroom. You can get up and walk round, can't you? Just shift the bed from the door.

She said, "Tow me back."

I got a ship and towed her back and got on the shore, and when I got her on the shore, I put her in a tent, and just as I was leaving the tent, she put her hand out and said, "You better massage my leg."

I said, "If I go in there and massage your leg, I shall get the sack."

Well, I still got the sack. I came out!

There were eight women in a boat and one was expecting a happy event. The other seven wanted to help her, but they were all in the same boat.

They say "you can't mix business with pleasure". I know a few girls who are doing it all right … in Brighton, anyway.

The Cheeky Chappie said, "I tell some old jokes..."

Did you see in the paper, the women are doing the men's jobs now? All the women are doing it now. 'Ere! No, shut up. No, well, it's not nice. Now in Brighton there's a woman. She's cleaning windows. It's a man's job, 'isn't it? There she was right on top of a ladder. Five storeys up she were. They say it's unlucky to walk under a ladder – 'Ere, I took a chance.

Now, ladies and gentlemen, there were four wrens standing on the station, Victoria Station, and they were all crying. So I said, "Come and have a cup of tea." So I took them into a café to have a cup of tea and the waitress brought the tea and I said to the girls, "Which one's going to be mother?" And they all started crying again.

I went to a nudist camp. I've never been in one before and I saw the fellow who was in charge. I said, "How do you keep the men away from the women?"

"Oh," he said. "It's easy. We put all the women on one side of the hedge and all the men on the other side of the hedge."

I said, "I bet there's a lot of beating about the bush, isn't there?"

All Good Stuff, Lady!

The Cheeky Chappie said, "Would you like to play a round?"

Tee-time with the Cheeky Chappie

Now, to get away from the wife I took up golf, and one morning a girl was standing on the tee. Oh dear! And I said, "Would you like to play a round?"

And she said, "Yes." So I did and she smacked my face.

I said, "What's that for?"

She said, "That's for nothing. Now do something."

"This one'll kill you!"

There was a young man, a young man playing golf, playing golf with a young lady. And he said, "My name's Peter, but I'm not a saint."

She said, "My name's Mary, but I'm not a, a ver-, ver-, not a very good player."

"Now 'ere's one."

Brand new balls – a handicap

I said to the chap that was near me, "Would you like a game?" And he said, "Yes." Now he put down a brand new ball and he hit this ball almost out of sight, and when we got there we couldn't find it. So he said, "Don't bother with it. It's all right. Leave it. We'll go to the next tee." At the next tee, he put down another brand new ball. He hit that and it went into the river.

He goes right across the course and the water was taking the ball away. He couldn't find it. At the next tee he put down another brand new ball and he lost that.

I said, "Jim, why don't you put down an old ball now and again when you come to these kind of hazards?" And he said, "I've never had one."

The Cheeky Chappie said, "I got on a bus..."

Asking for trouble

I got on a bus the other day and I sat inside and the conductress came in and said, "No smoking inside."

I said, "I'm not smoking."

She said, "You've got a cigarette in your mouth."

I said, "I know. I got my shoes on but I'm not walking."

She said, "Do you want to get me into trouble?"

I said, "Yes, what time do you finish?"

And just then we had a head-on crash with another bus and the bus turned right over and all the people were lying around in the road there. And a policeman came along and I got out of my bus and went over to him, I said, "Has the insurance man been?" He said, "No." I said, "Can I lie down with the others?"

The Girl

It's a little girl ... she keeps on biting her nails and her mother said, "Stop biting your nails because you know what'll happen to you?"

"What will happen to me?"

"You won't half get fat, if you bite your nails."

She said, "I won't bite them anymore, Mum." The mother took her shopping, got on a bus and there was a fellow sitting in the corner, weighing about twenty stone, and she said, "Mama, I'll get like that, won't I?"

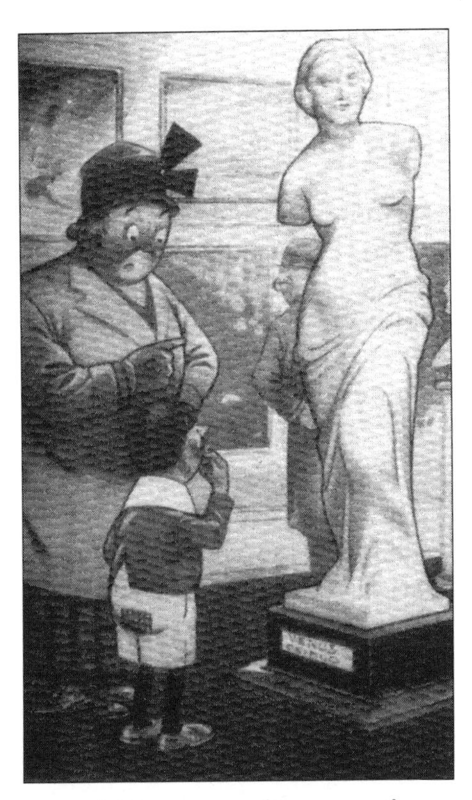

Stop biting your finger nails - you see what'll happen to you if you don't!

And she said, "You'll get worse than that if you bite them."

"Well, I won't bite them anymore."

And after shopping, they got on another bus and there was a blonde sitting in the corner. She's carrying a bit of weight as well ...

That's what I like about you, you're so quick!

And the kiddie kept looking at the blonde, and the blonde kept looking at the kiddie. And the blonde couldn't stand it any longer, so she said, "Do you know me?"

And the kiddie said, "No, but I know what you've been doing!"

"Come 'ere! Listen, listen!"

An 'affare' at a bus stop

I saw a nice woman standing at a bus stop and I said, "Are you waiting for a bus?"

She said, "No, I'm waiting for the fare."

I said, "Have you got the time?"

She said, "Yes."

I said, "Well I haven't. I can't afford it!"

She shall have music

I saw a girl standing at a bus stop. I said, "How do you do?"

She said, "How do I do what?"

I said, "Please yourself."

She said, "I'm not a pick up."

I said, "I wasn't going to pick you up."

So we sat down and we waited for the bus and I noticed on her leg she had a violin tattooed on her leg and on her other leg she had a bow, and every time she crossed her legs, it started to play Don't Fence Me In.

Two girls were talking on a bus. "Are you wearing those lovely new undies?" "No, I'm saving them." "For a rainy day?" "No, for a windy day."

The Cheeky Chappie said, "I was standing in a pub and a chap said to me . . ."

"Max, you look fed up."

I said, "Yes, I *am* fed up. I've just heard the news that I'm a daddy and I'm a bit worried about it."

He said, "What does the wife think about it?"

I said, "That's what I'm worried about – she doesn't know."

Gin and what's it?

Then a posh fellow walked in and he said to the barmaid, "A gin and angostura." So the barmaid not being too bright like – just started the game, you see. So she gave him the gin and said, "That's two and six."

He said, "Well, what about the angostura?"

"Oh," she said, "You're a stranger here, aren't you?"

He said, "Yes."

She said, "It's down the passage on the right."

Two sailors and two girls walked into the pub and the boss said, "I'm not serving those two girls. They are doubtful characters."

The sailor said, "Doubtful, they're stone wall certs. What are you talking about?"

My goodness

Now a chap walked in. He'd had plenty. He was carrying a right load this fellow. He looked like making two trips, this one. So I said, "Hello Charlie, what are you having?"

He said, "I'll have a whisky."

I said, "How's the wife?"

He said, "Oh dear, she's fallen down the stairs and broken her leg."

I said, "I'm sorry to hear that."

He said, "I'll be glad when they shout time, so I can go home and pick her up."

Drunk again

Just then a chap walked into my pub and I thought to myself, "I know you." I looked at him and thought, "I know you" and I looked at him and said, "Hello Russell, you've changed. The last time I saw you, you had a black beard and now you're without. I've never seen such a change in anyone. You *have* changed. If I remember rightly, you stood about six foot four. Well, you can't be more than five feet now. You *have* changed. There's no doubt about it. And you were so thin. And look at you now, you're about sixteen stone. I've never seen anything like it."

He said, "Listen, for your benefit, I don't know who you are." He said, "and I've never had a beard," he said. "And I was never six foot four and my name is not Russell."

So I said, "Oh, and you've changed your name as well, eh?"

Well, after we had a few drinks, I went home. I gave the wife a kiss and she said, "Drunk again."

I said, "That's all right, I'll talk to you again when you're sober."

She hit me in the mouth and I sobered up like a bank holiday. I wanted to be nice to her and I started calling her names like my little lamb, my little pet, my little deer, and the animals started to get bigger and bigger.

She said, "I don't know why I ever married you."

I said, "You married me, because you couldn't get anyone else."

She said, "Yes I could, I could have got anybody I liked."

I said, "Why didn't you?"

She said, "I didn't like anybody."

Stringing along with you

I went into a hotel the other day and into the bar, and as I was standing by the bar there was a fellow eating olives on a string.

I said, "What are you eating them like that for?"

He said, "I may not like them."

I met a pal of mine the other day. I said, "Charlie, they tell me you're married now."

He said, "That's right."

I said, "Then you know what's what?"

He said, "What do you mean?"

I said, "If you're married, you must know what's what."

He said, "I think you're crazy."

He started walking home and as he started walking home, he said to himself, Now you're married you know what's what. When he got home that night, he got into the bedroom. The wife was in bed, so he took all his clothes off and he switched the light out. He didn't want to get out again, see. He was in the dark and he was feeling around in the dark. And all of a sudden he said, "What's that?" And the wife said, "What's what?" **'Ere!**

And there it was on the mantelpiece all the time!

The trouble is, I don't know the value of money. I went to a barmaid and said, "If I gave you five pounds less ten per cent, what would you take off?"

She said, "You'd be surprised." In this weather!

Poet's

Corner

"Listen! I'll tell you what I want to do now, a recitation, listen!"

It was a terrible night in the desert.
We were putting the camels to bed,
When one of them sat with his legs crossed,
Scratching the back of his head.
The perfume which came from the camels
Filled everyone with delight.
You could always find them by their sensor
No matter how dark the night.

We eat lots of sand in the desert,
It doesn't hurt you a bit.
You know why we eat sand in the desert,
Because the girls like the men full of grit.

Princess charming

There was a little girl
Who had a little curl
Right in the middle of her forehead;
And when she was good, she was very, very good,
And when she was bad she was very, very popular.

The Cheeky Chappie said, "I better stay on the blue book, 'eh? I think so, all right?"

Two wicked squires

She was but a village maiden,
Who's to say she was to blame?
But alas a wicked squire
Took away her honest name.
So she journeyed up to London
Seeking to forget her shame,
When another wicked squire
Took away her other name.

Adam and Eve in the Garden dwelt,
They were so happy and jolly.
I wonder how they would have felt,
If all the leaves had been holly!

Jack and Jill went up the hill
On a Sunday morning.
Jill came running down again
She heard the gypsy's warning.

And again!

Jack and Jill went up the hill
Just like two cock linnets.
Jill came down with half-a-crown,
She wasn't up there two... ***'Ere!***

Ain't it ni-ice

We met at a cocktail party. She said, "How do you do."
It was New Year's Eve so I said, "a Happy New Year to you."
We sat down to dine –
A bottle of wine –
Then we started on gin.
It was love at first sight,
And, oh, what a night!
We were letting the New Year in.
She said, "See me home."
In her doorway we stood, Big Ben was striking two.
I said, "It's too late for me to go home,
I'd better stay here with you."
I kept hugging her; she kept hugging me;
I was as drunk as can be.
And to make matters worse,
She lost her purse,
And inside her purse was her key.
I said, "Try my key, perhaps we can get in with that."
I could feel the effects of the gin.
As she opened the door, she fell on the mat
And cried "Meredith, we're in!"

But, oh, what a lark,
We were both in the dark;
Where the gas meter was she forgot.
And wasn't it strange,
We couldn't find any change.
If we could, we couldn't find the slot.
Then she whispered, "You'll have to sleep on the floor."
A pillow she placed 'neath my head.
But I can't make it out from that day to this,
How it was that I fell out of bed …

Mary from the Dairy?

Mary had a little lamb
Who acted very silly.
She plucked the wool from off its back
And smacked its Piccadilly.

Mary had a little bear
To which she was so kind.
I've often seen her bear in front …

"I'll get on to the next joke here."

Jack struts in

One day a girl she was bathing,
The maid said, "Here comes Mr Tree."
She said, "All right bring him to me.
He's quite safe – the poor chap can't see."
She stood there like a beautiful Venus,
When into the bathroom walked Jack.
He said, "I've just come to tell you.
Today I've got my eyesight back!"

I stood on the bridge at midnight.
A tramp came tramping along.
The clock didn't strike the hour
But the tramp stopped me pretty strong.
He told me he had twelve children
I said, "Twelve children that's pretty tough.
He said, "Could you do something for me?"
I said, "Blimey aren't twelve children enough?"

There was a young woman from Devizes
She had tits of different sizes.
One was so small
It was no use at all,
The other so big it won prizes.

The Pure Gold of the Music Hall

"Music Halls... they don't make 'em any more, Duck!"

I went to a music 'all the other week. I took the wife, I took the wife and we sat in the front row and two comedians came on the stage. I've never heard such filth in all my life ... And I've heard some; I've heard some ... But the gags they came out with, oh dear! I've never heard anything like it. And one comedian turned and said, "How's the wife?"

He said, "I left her in bed smoking." He said, "How's yours?"

"I can't even tell her the answer, isn't it funny?"

There's a fellow working at the docks and he said to the governor, "Could I have the afternoon off?"

He said, "Not Saturday afternoon, you get double pay."

The fellow said, "I'm not concerned about double pay. I want to go home, the wife's expecting a happy event."

He said, "Well in that case you had better go then."

So he went home and returned on Monday and the governor said, "All right?"

He said, "Yes it turned out all right." He said, "What is it, a boy or a girl?"

He said, "We won't know till about nine months time."

"This one'll kill you!"

A father had two sons and a daughter. One boy went to Oxford; the other one went to Cambridge. And the girl, she wasn't any good either. One day the boy came home from Oxford. He said, "Dad, I'm in trouble with the girlfriend and unless I give her a thousand pounds, she's going to sue me."

His father said, "I've only got two thousand pounds, but for the good name of the family, you shall have a thousand pounds."

The following day the other boy walked in from Cambridge. He said, "Dad, I'm in trouble with the girlfriend. Unless I give her a thousand pounds, she's going to sue me."

His father said, "I've only got a thousand pounds but for the good name of the family, you shall have a thousand pounds."

A few days later the daughter walked in. She said, "Dad, I'm in trouble.

He said, "That's better – this is where we collect."

"Simmer down!"

The Cheeky Chappie said, "He's a boy, isn't he 'eh? Hope so. Well how can you tell? You can't tell. It can change overnight."

La-de-dah-de-da

Candid camera?

Now there's a soldier, a soldier standing in the dock. The judge is at the back, the jury over there, the defending counsel down here. The judge said to the soldier, "This is a very serious case. We shall have to hold this in camera."

And the soldier said, "What does that mean?"

And the judge said, "It won't make any difference to you. The jury, they know what it means. The defending counsel, he knows what it means and I know what it means. Clear the court."

He said to the soldier, "Tell me exactly what happened."

So the soldier said, "Well," he said, "I met this girl and she asked me to see her home. She told me she lived out in the country. Well, I took her the short way across the field and, when I got to the centre of the field, I don't know what came over me but I got hold of her, no rough stuff, that came later, see. And I started to kiss her and she passed out, she passed right out. Then after that it was all la-de-dah-de-da."

And the judge said, "All *what*?"

The soldier said, "All la-de-dah-de-da."

And the judge said, "What does that mean?"

The soldier said, "Well then, the jury, they know what it means, and the defending counsel, he knows what it means, and if you'd been there with your camera, you'd have known, too."

"Its all clever stuff you know, clever, inn' it, clever? No rubbish, no rubbish."

Two dogs talking and one said to the other, "Have you done your pools?"

The other one said, "No, I just missed the post."

Listen, lady, we men are just like children. We prefer blondes because we're afraid of the dark.

You must have heard about the absent-minded nudist who went out with his trousers on!

"Listen, listen, listen! Are you listening? Right."

The cattle market

Father and son, the boy would be 8 or 9, he may be 10, we don't know – who cares anyway? His father took him to a cattle show on Saturday afternoon where the farmers were buying the bulls and cows, mostly bulls, when all of a sudden the little boy saw a farmer go up to a bull and the farmer started feeling the bull, all along the back he was feeling it, all down and all round, feeling all over. And the little boy said, "Daddy what's he doing?"

And his father told him. His father said, "He's feeling to see if there is any meat on it. If there's any meat on it, he's going to buy it."

The boy thanked his father for telling him. Two or three weeks later, the boy went to see his father at breakfast. The father asked him what he wanted. The boy said, "I think the butler wants to buy the cook."

"Which would you like? You like the Blue Book or the White Book? You like 'em both, don't you? Listen!"

Keep it in the family

A soldier had been abroad for about seven years and while he was away his wife had been unfaithful to him. She had a baby. So he was coming home, you see. So she said to the woman next door, "Charlie's coming home and he doesn't know anything about this baby, I wish you'd take it. And when he goes back, I'll take it back from you."

She said, "That's all right with me."

So, sure enough Charlie came home and when he was home, after he had his lunch he said, "Well, now let's have a look at it."

She said, "What are you talking about?"

He said, "I know all about it; you don't have to kid me."

So the wife thought, hallo, the woman next door must have told him. So she went next door and she said, "Did you tell my husband about my baby?"

The woman said, "Well, what could I do? He asked me and I couldn't do anything about it, so I told him."

She said, "That's all right. You can keep it – because it's your old man's anyway."

The Cheeky Chappie said, "You can't help liking him, can you?"

We had a burglary in our street. I chased the burglar down the high street, past the fire station, past the butcher's, past the Co-op, and eventually I caught him by the cobblers.

The Cheeky Chappie's cleanest joke ever!

The day in the life of a film star. She gets up at six o'clock in the morning, takes a bath, goes for a five mile walk, comes back and takes another bath, goes off to the studio, does two hours work, takes another bath, comes back in the evening, has a cup of coffee and takes another bath. And you must agree with me, ladies and gentlemen, that's about the cleanest joke I've ever cracked.

Swear-box

There was this boy who had just come down from Oxford – that's the place where they have a school for illiterates. They learn to speak proper, like wot I does. He swore with every other word. It did upset his old man. He was a clergyman, see.

"This is the house of God," he said. "Promise me that every time you swear you'll give the person nearest to you a sum of money."

Next morning, the boy was going down the stairs when he tripped and fell over the mat.

"Who put that bloody mat there?" he said.

"I did," said the new maid. She was a nice bit of overtime 'n' all. Then the boy, he remembered his promise, fished in his pocket and all he had on him was his wallet. He had to give the maid a quid.

"Cor blimey!" she said. "Like father, like son. Where do you want it – in the front room or up in the attic?"

Tit for tat

A fellow took his wife to Paris. There's a novelty to start with – it's foolish, like taking coal to Newcastle. No, I mean they've got a lot of coal up there, haven't they?

He took his wife to Paris and they were walking along the boulevard one morning, when, all of a sudden, she saw a hat in a shop window. She said, "John, I like the hat; buy it for me."

He said, "No, I spent a lot of money, I'll buy a hat, when we get back to town."

She said, "No, buy this one, because I like it; it will suit me."

He said, "No, don't waste any time, ducky, lets go for a walk."

So they went for a walk, and as they were going along he saw a red lamp. So he turned to the wife, he said, "You still fancy the hat?"

She said, "Yes."

He said, "There's a £1; go and get it. Take your time."

No, no, what he meant was get a good one, a good one.

Listen!

She went to get the hat, he went towards the red lamp, and when he got there it turned green.

"Now this is a funny thing..."

A fellow said to me, he said, "Max, do you believe in the transmigration of souls?"

I said, "What do you mean?"

He said, "When you die, you come back something entirely different, you see."

I said, "No, I don't believe that."

And, as I was walking home, I heard a voice say, "Hello, Max," and I turned round and it was a white horse, see. And he said, "Don't you remember me? I died a few weeks ago and I came back as a horse and I'm pulling this coal cart around all day long." And he said, "I'm sick and tired of it."

I said, "Why don't you tell the boss about it?"

He said, "I should think so. If he knew I could talk, he would have me shouting 'coal' as well!"

Box clever

A deaf and dumb man got married and his wife made him wear boxing gloves in bed. That was to stop him talking in his sleep.

Everything happens to me

What do you think of this hat? A present from the wife. The only present I had this year. I came home unexpectedly and there it was on the table.

The good companions

An old couple were sitting around a fire, sitting around the fire listening to the wireless, when all of a sudden the old man passed out. She said, "What's the matter Jim?"

He said, "Jean, I was thinking, its our golden wedding today and wouldn't it be lovely if we could go to Bournemouth and stay in the same hotel as we did fifty years ago today?"

She said, "Why shouldn't we?" She was game. So they got on a tandem and away they went and they got to Bournemouth.

She said, "Here we are in the same room, in the same surroundings, the same pictures on the wall, everything the same as it stood fifty years ago today." She said, "Don't you remember how eager you were to kiss me? You didn't give me time to get my stockings off."

Listen, listen, listen!

He said, "You'll have plenty of time tonight to knit yourself a pair."

Body parts

A chap was telling me about his wedding night. He said his wife took off her wooden leg and put it in the top drawer. Then she took off her false arm and put that in the top drawer. Then she took off her wig and put that in the top drawer. He said, "I just stood there wondering whether I should sleep in the bed or get into the top drawer."

I'm no donkey, you silly ass!

This feller had a donkey, and it was going to be 21, and he didn't know what to get it for its birthday. Straight up. *No, listen!* So he asked the donkey and it said (there's a fine thing – it was a talking donkey, you see), it said, "Haven't you any feelings? Here I am slaving away for you for 21 years and never a spot of female company; so that's what I want."

So the feller felt bad. Well, you would, wouldn't you? And he looked everywhere for a female donkey he could hire for the night. But the best he could do was a lady zebra. So that was all fixed up and when the birthday came, he put the zebra in with the donkey. Next morning the feller hurried in to ask his donkey did everything go all right.

"All right. No, it bloody well didn't," said the donkey. "I spent all night trying to get her pyjamas off!"

Hard to please

I asked my dad. I said, "Dad – is it hard to please a woman?"

He said, "It is if it isn't."

"WHAT YOU NEED IS SOMETHING TO MAKE IT HARD!"

Confessions of a Cheeky Chappie

"Listen, listen!"

Now when I started in this business many years ago, I started in the circus. I'm not a stereotype comedian, don't think that for one moment. When I come out here, I don't know what I am going to say, but I wouldn't say I don't care, because I do care. I started in Billy Smart's Circus, not the Billy Smart of today, but his father who is much older than me. And I remember one day he said to me, "Maxie, would you like to be a lion tamer?" I said, "I've no desire." He said, "There's money in it." I said, "What do I have to do?" He said, "All you have got to do is to walk in the lion's cage and put your head in its mouth." I said, "I should think so." He said, "Are you scared?" I said, "I'm not scared, I'm just careful." He said, "I shouldn't be scared of that lion." He said, "That lion's as tame as a kitten. It was brought up on milk." I said, "So was I, but I eat meat!"

So they advertised for a lion tamer and a beautiful blonde came along like they are today, you've seen them, well out in front, a lovely roll desk. And that's a lot of madam and all – that's the ironing board stuck up there. So he said to this blonde, "Would you go in this cage?" She said, "I'll go in because I'm a lion tamer." And she walked into the cage and, as she walked into the cage, the lion made a dash for her. She thought quick and undid her zip and all her clothes fell off and she stood there, as naked as she came into the world, and the lion, he stopped. Then he started to walk towards her and, when he got near enough, he started to kiss her. And he kissed her all over and the gov'ner said, "Would you do that?"

I said, "Yes, get the lion out!"

The Book on Etiquette and Manners

Now simmer down. I don't want you people to mix me up with these people behind me this week, because every act on the programme this week, Oxford and Cambridge, myself a self-taught lad. A self-taught lad in every respect and I owe my success to this book, *Etiquette and Manners*. And you can be as well educated as I am, lady, for the price of sixpence. You can get them in Marks or Woolworth's, *Etiquette and Manners*. It tells you what to do, what not to do, when, and very likely according to how you're feeling. How you feeling, lady? And I might tell you; you can't go wrong with a book like this, lady. Impossible to go wrong with a book like this ... I'll get you another book, duck ... It says in the book, listen, 'When you're in company, take your hat off'. I think I'm in the wrong company this week. I keep mine on. It says in the book, 'How to eat fish and where to spit the bones'. That's a bit of a novelty, isn't it?

There's one, there's one . . .

I shall never forget when I went to a party. There were fifty of us at the party and we sat at the table and the maid came in and she said, "Would you like a serviette?"

I thought a serviette was a napkin, see. So I looked in the book and it's right. It *is* a napkin. It tells you where to put it...

"You can't go wrong with a book like this!"

"Etiquette and Manners - it's all clever stuff"

How to drink a cocktail and what to do with the cherry. 'Ere listen. I'll tell you. Its all clever stuff you know, isn't it? All clever. You can't go wrong with it.

It says in the book, it says in the book, when you're walking with a young lady, walk on the outside, always on the outside. When you're walking with the wife, right over the other side of the road.

Max's good fortune

I'm the happiest lad in the world. I've got no troubles. Do you know why I am happy? Today I'm a daddy. After 18 years I'm a daddy. And before the happy event, my wife went to see a fortune-teller. The fortune-teller told her, "If it's a boy, the father will die. If it's a girl, the mother will die."

I've got a letter here from my mother-in-law on my father's side. I'll read it to you. "Dear Max, the wife has presented you with a lovely bouncing baby boy, both doing well."

That shows you what the fortune-teller knows. Here am I strong as a lion, game for anything. She goes on to say, "PS. Sorry to say the milkman dropped dead this morning."

The Cheeky Chappie said, "Now there's a funny thing."

No go, go - no can, can

I said to my father, I said, "Dad, I want to go to Paris. I want to see the Folies-Bergère." He said, "You're not going. You might see something there you shouldn't see." And he was right. I went. I saw *him* there.

Voulez-vous promenade?

I went to Paris last week. I went into a café and sat next to a beautiful French girl. Now I couldn't speak French and she couldn't speak English, so I drew a bottle on the menu and the waiter brought a bottle of wine. Then I drew another bottle of wine and he brought another bottle of wine. And as time went on in the early hours of the morning, she drew a bed on the menu. Now I couldn't make out how she knew I was in the furniture business.

"'Ere, I got one"

Not half!!

I said to my father, "Dad, I want to get married." He said, "All right Son, who do you want to marry?"

"I'd like to marry Miss Green," I said.

He said, "You can't."

I said, "Why not?"

He said, "She's your half-sister." He said, "When I was a lad, I had a bike and I got around a bit."

I said, "All right, I'll marry Miss White."

He said, "You can't, she's your half-sister, forget about it."

Well, I was a bit despondent and I walked around, and my mum said to me, "What's wrong with you?"

"Well," I said, "I said to dad, I wanted to marry Miss Green, but he said I couldn't, because she's my half-sister. All right, I said, I'll marry Miss White, and he said I can't she's my half-sister."

She said, "Look, go and marry which one you like – he's not your father anyway."

"The girls I like"

There were these two girls. They visited me backstage and, as they left the theatre, one of them said, "Doesn't he dress nice?" And the other said, "Yes, and so quickly."

I was found on a doorstep. "An orphan?" "No, a step child."

A monologue from The Cheeky Chappie

Ladies and gentlemen, I'd like to say this if I may. It's not really a speech but I've been a bit of a bad lad in my time, and I remember many years ago my brother and I, who is two years younger than me, we went out together and after two or three weeks I said, "Johnny, I've got a confession to make."

He said, "Go in and tell your father."

I went into the drawing room to see me dad. He was sitting in a deckchair. I said, "Dad, I've got a confession to make."

He said, "What's it, Son?" And I didn't like to tell him. He said, "Tell me, who was it?" And I wouldn't tell him. He said, "Was it Mrs Brown?" I said, "No, no." He said, "Was it Mrs Mitchell?" I said, "No." I wouldn't crack on, you see. He said, "Was it Mrs Smith?" I said, "No." He said, "Get out of the room." He was disgusted with me.

I walked out of the room and my brother said, "How did you get on? Did he forgive you?"

I said, "No, but he gave me three very good addresses."

I've just come clean from Paris - and it takes a bit of doing to come clean from Paris.

A Trunk Call

There's a woman, a woman washing clothes down by the river and she was sitting down, well, sitting down on her laundry, see. And all of a sudden an elephant came down to get a drink, and he walked behind her and must have touched her with his trunk, you see. So without turning round she said, "I don't know who you are, man, but I'm here every Monday, Wednesday and Friday."

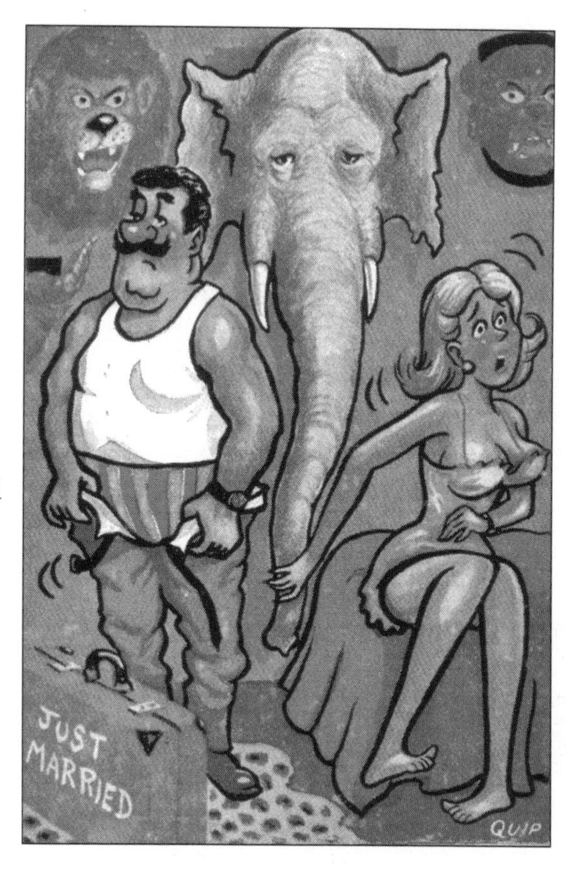

The Cheeky Chappie said, "There's no one like me - there'll never be another!"

The Cheeky Chappie says, "Do you fancy me, girl? You do? Well, you've got good taste."

Fools in paradise?

I had a shocking dream the other night, a shocking dream. I dreamt three of my pals and myself went to Hell. And when we got down there the devil said to the first one, "What are you doing here?"

He said, "I don't know. I haven't done anything wrong. I've never neglected the wife. I never go with women. And I don't smoke. I don't know why I'm here."

The devil said to the other one, "What about you?"

He said, "Well, I'm the same as him. I've never neglected the wife. I don't go with women. I don't smoke. I don't drink. I don't know why I'm here." And the third exactly the same.

Then he turned to me and said, "What about you, Miller?"

I said, "I'm entitled to be here. I've done everything wrong. I've neglected the wife. I've gone with women."

He said, "You're the boy I'm looking for. Do you know what I'm going to do?"

I said, "No."

He said, "I'm going to burn the other three and you and I are going to have a good night out!"

I can't do it, you can't do it and the dairymaid can't do it. What's that? Milk chocolate!

"Listen, listen! Is there no end to his cleverness?"

Now I started courting when I was seventeen. I was in the kitchen brushing my hair back, putting on a clean collar three inches high; the collar looked like I had my ears off, and my mother said, "Where are you going?"

I said, "I'm going courting."

She said, "You're going to bed." Dead wicked, dead wicked me mother. What a crafty woman, eh? She said, "Get up those stairs." She'd send me to bed with no supper.

I said, "I've had no supper."

She said, "You'll get no supper, but a piece of bread and butter, one slice."

My father came in. He said, "Where's Maxie?"

She said, "I caught him in the kitchen making himself up. He was going courting. I sent him to bed."

He said, "What?"

She said, "I sent him to bed. I gave him a slice of bread and butter."

He said, "Where's the frying pan?"

She said, "You're not going to hit him with that, are you?"

He said, "No, I'm going to fry him a piece of steak. He can't go courting on bread and butter." *Now, listen!*

The Cheeky Chappie said, "They don't make 'em like this anymore, lady. When I'm dead and gone, the game's over."

© Hulton Getty

"I'm ready for bed now. Anybody?"

The MMAS Max-word puzzle

MAX-WORD PUZZLE

Across

1 'Hello My Darlings,' said this Charlie
7 Something special about this audience
8 Could members of the Water Rats be called this, perhaps?
9 Holborn, Hackney and Croydon all had 'em!
11 Sir Jim OBE would be suited in this row
13 Clapton, Beck and Page started with this 60's group
15 Max would stare and peer together to achieve these witty routines
19 Mixed up net boy makes 21st century BBC executive
21 Sounds just like your father in France to introduce a show
23 Unlikely Max got into a cage with one of these females!
24 When Max appeared on Radio Luxembourg he was often interrupted by these
25 The man in black was this Valentine

Down

1 One of Jack's famous sisters
2 Dame Vera freely offered her services to troops on this sort of service
3 Namely Phil and Don shared this
4 Partnering Eric Morcambe was indeed
5 Not much cover atoll for the girl, eh, Max?
6 Max Miller, Dan Leno, G.H. Elliott – Music Hall .....
10 This Albert was famous for his tram driver impression!
12 HMTQ follows Max's biographer for this Spring Bank Holiday
14 Max broke these in theatres, and made a few in his time
16 Max would add these to some pears and soon be on the up
17 Max would often make a quick escape from this house
18 This 'B' cargo ship ended up on Brighton Beach in 1980
20 Some herb, Mr Fawlty
22 I'm taken away from the sister of 1 Down or .....

All about us . . .

The Max Miller Appreciation Society (MMAS) was founded in 1999 to celebrate the life and achievements of Max Miller, "The Cheeky Chappie". Max was born and raised in Brighton, where the Society meets, and he lived almost his whole life there. MMAS has grown in strength, keeping alive Max's legacy and remembering "the good old days" of Music Hall and Variety. Since 1999 the Society has achieved many successes:

- Unveiling blue plaques on premises where Max lived, at Ashcroft house in Shoreham (1946 to 1950) and 160 Marine Parade, Brighton (1936 to 1946).
- Creating and maintaining a successful and informative website with links to the BBC and other related sites. "Hits" now exceed 100,000.
- Publication of a lively quarterly magazine "There'll Never Be Another!" featuring reminiscences and stories about Max and the variety theatre.
- Publication of *The Max Miller Appreciation Society Blue Book,* celebrating Max's humour, which is now in its second edition. You are holding it in your hand – hold it carefully!
- Annual convention weekend, featuring a film show, guided tour, annual dinner and a special variety show for members.
- Promoting a successful six-month Max Miller exhibit at Brighton & Hove Museum.
- Acting as a focal point for Max Miller memorabilia and merchandise for fans and supporters.
- Erection of a bronze statue of Max in the Royal Pavilion grounds, Brighton, unveiled by Sir Norman Wisdom, Roy Hudd OBE, June Whitfield DBE and George Melly during a memorable gala day.
- Mounting a successful permanent exhibition of Max memorabilia at Brighton's premier fish & chip shop, Bardsleys, ("The Cheeky Chippie") in Baker Street.
- Naming the "Max Miller Walk" on Brighton seafront in memory of the great man. The Society has "adopted" the Walk and is working with Brighton & Hove City Council to improve and add interest to the area.
- Arranging an occasional "Max Miller Garden Party" to raise funds for local and entertainment charities. By 2010, a sum in excess of £10,000 had been handed over to good causes.
- Promoting a series of variety shows intended to "bring back variety" to Brighton.

MAX-WORD PUZZLE ANSWERS

ACROSS:

1.DRAKE 7.INVITED 8.RATTERS 9.EMPIRES
11.SAVILE 13.YARDBIRDS 15.REPARTEES 19.YENTOB
21.COMPERE 23.LIONESS 24.ADVERTS 25.DYALL

DOWN:

1.DORIS 2.ACTIVE 3.EVERLY 4.WISE
5.BIKINI 6.LEGENDS 10.MODLEY 12.EASTER
14.RECORDS 16.APPLES 17.SECOND 18.ATHENA
20 BASIL 22.ELSE